Rudy's Secret CAP

by
Al Petitpas & Judy Van Raalte

Illustrations by Max Vento

A Publication of Springfield College

© Copyright 2009 by Al Petitpas and Judy Van Raalte
All rights reserved. No part of this book may be reproduced
in any form without permission in writing from the authors.

Springfield College (www.springfieldcollege.edu)
Max Vento (www.maxvento.blogspot.com www.actoraspirante.com)

Hi, my name is Rudy Brown and I play football, basketball, and baseball at North High.
When I was in the third grade, I was kind of fat and not very good at sports. But then I learned the secrets to being a smart player and a good student. Do you want to learn these secrets?

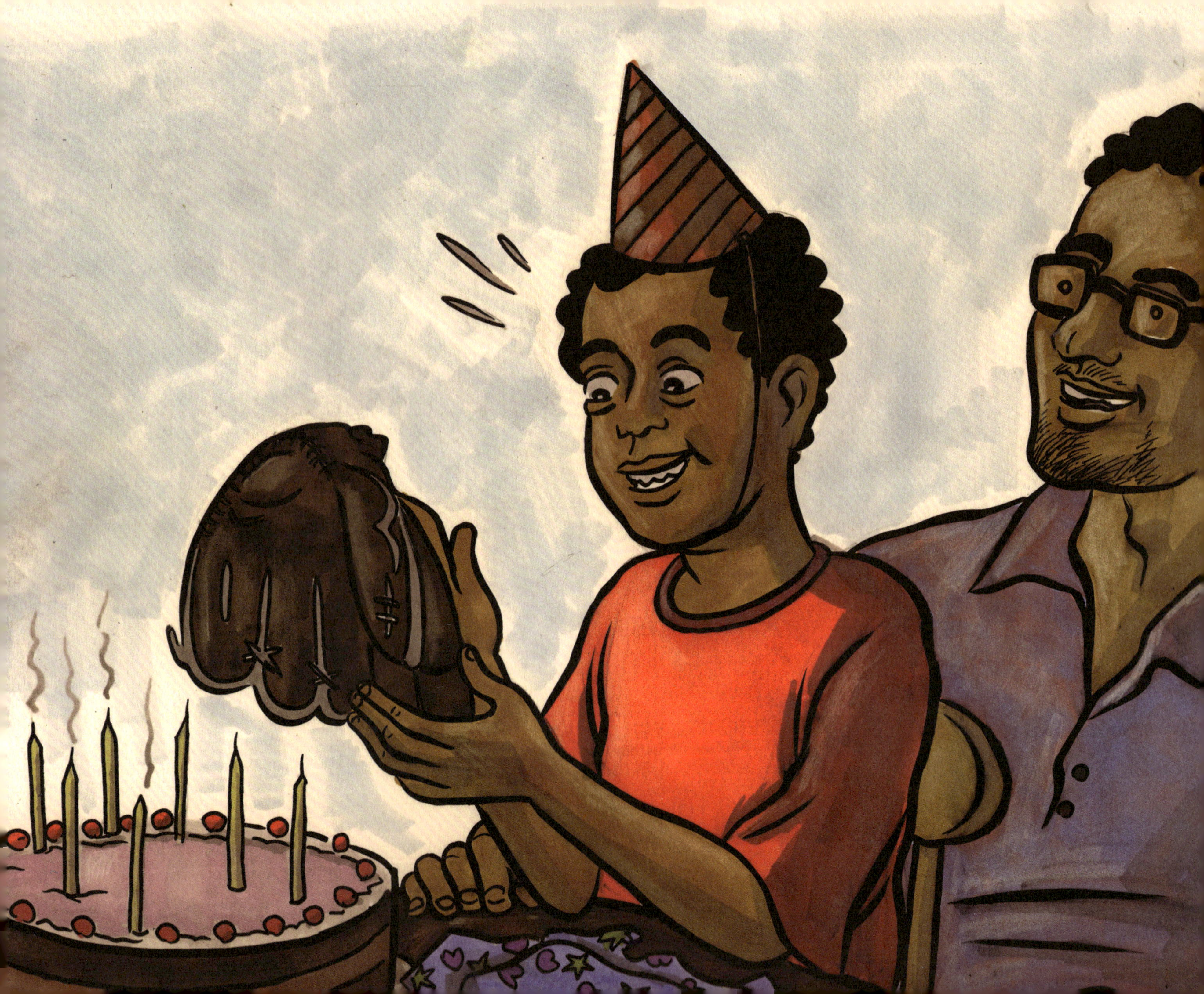

When I was eight years old, I got a baseball glove for my birthday. I was so happy that I couldn't wait to try it out.

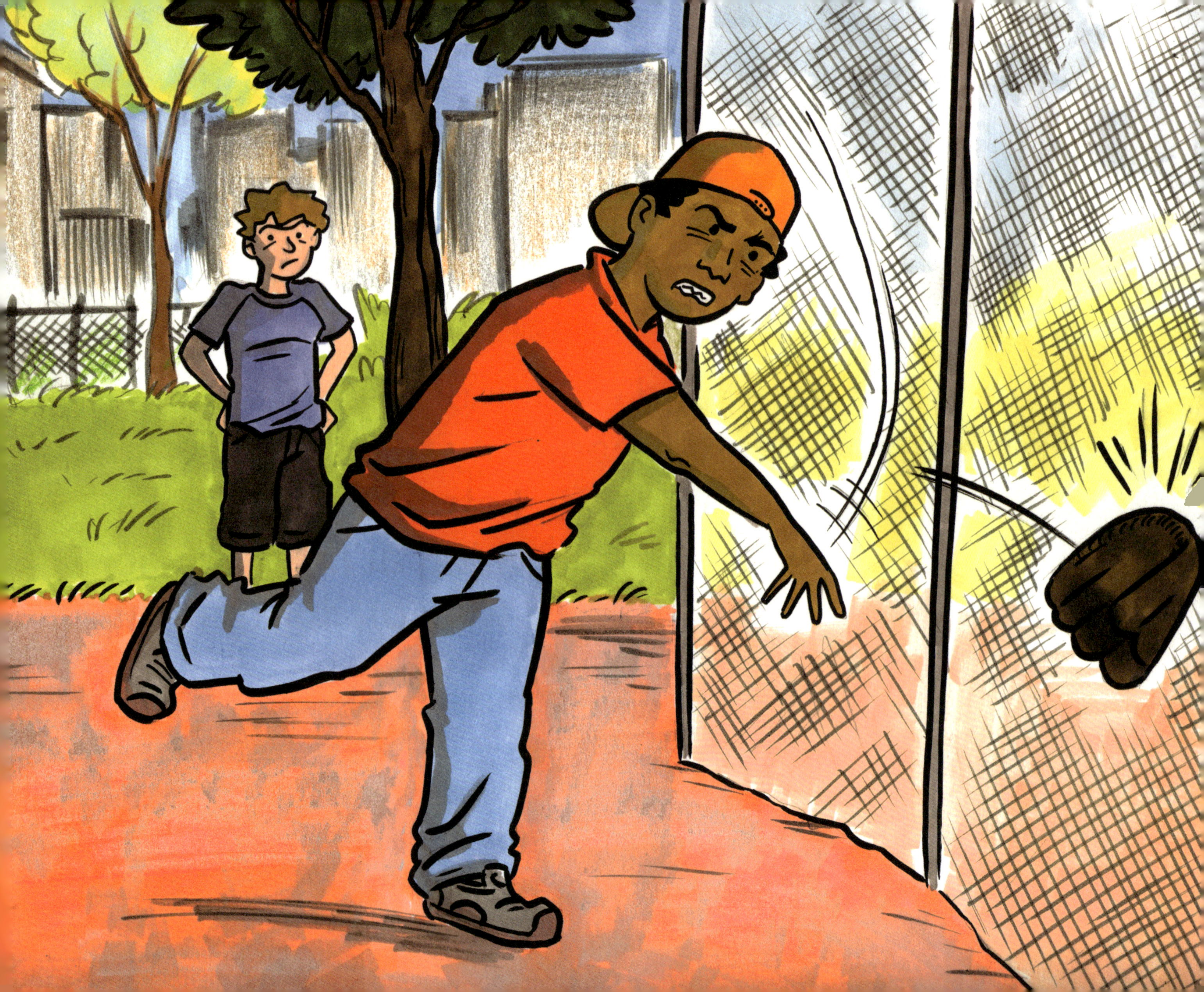

I ran to the park, and Carlos picked me to play on his team. When it came my turn to bat, I struck out. Next time up, I struck out again. The older kids started laughing at me. I got so mad, I threw my glove and took off for home.

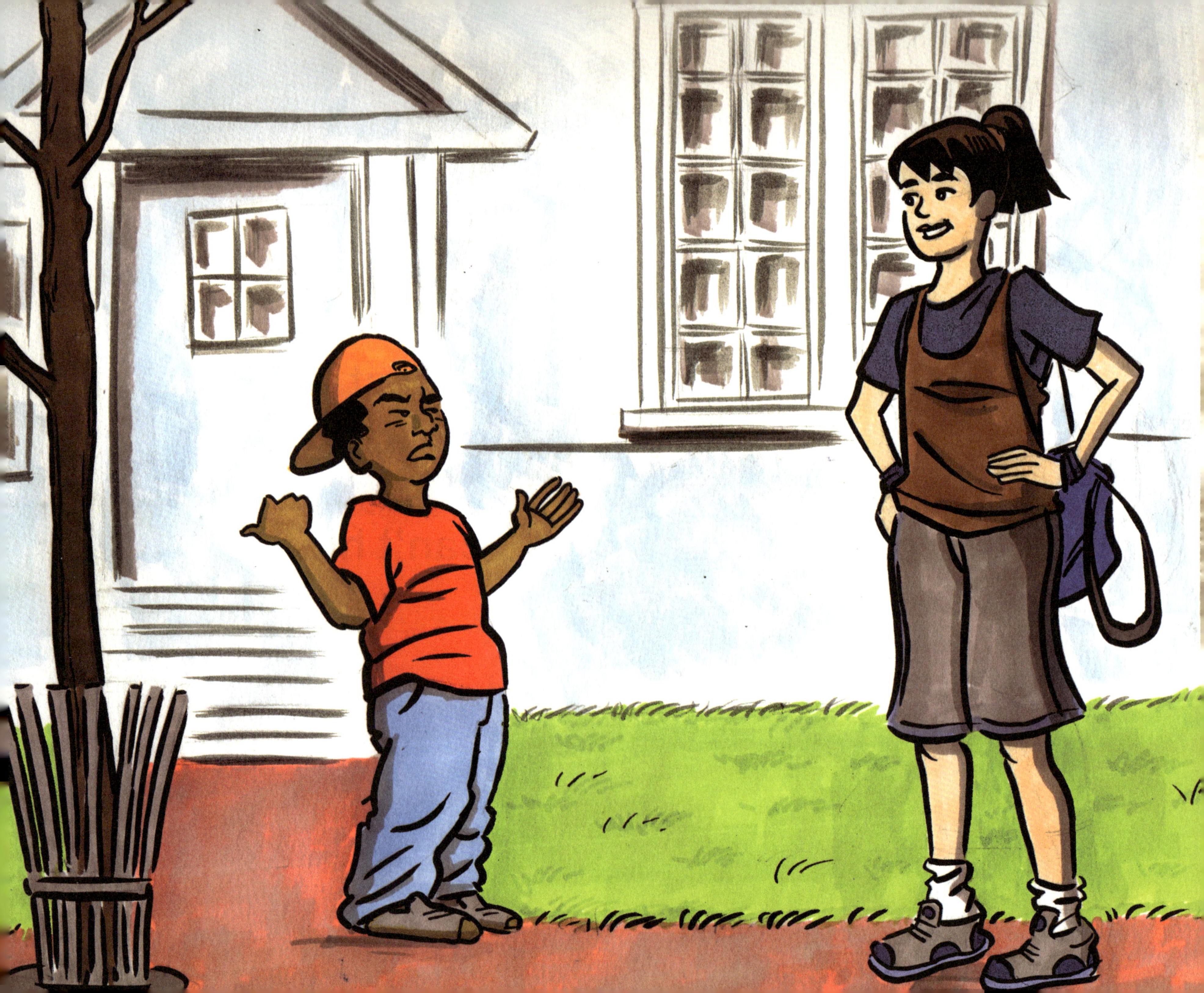

Crystal, who is practically the best basketball player in the whole city, caught up to me. "What's wrong?" she asked. "They said I was too fat, too slow, and I can't hit. I'm never going back."

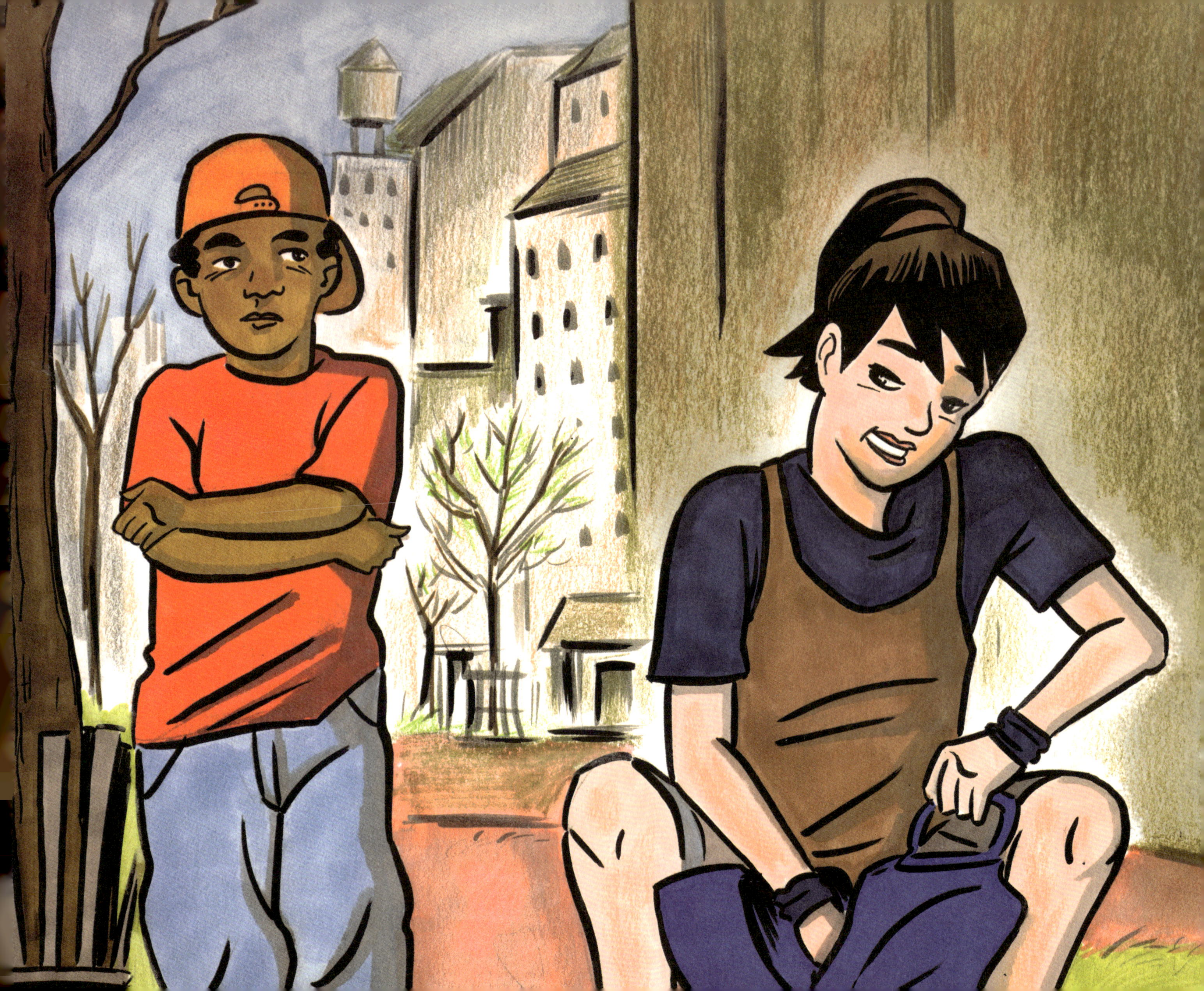

Crystal pulled a baseball hat out of her backpack. "This cap is the secret to my success," Crystal said.

I wondered, how could her old hat help me to be a good ball player?

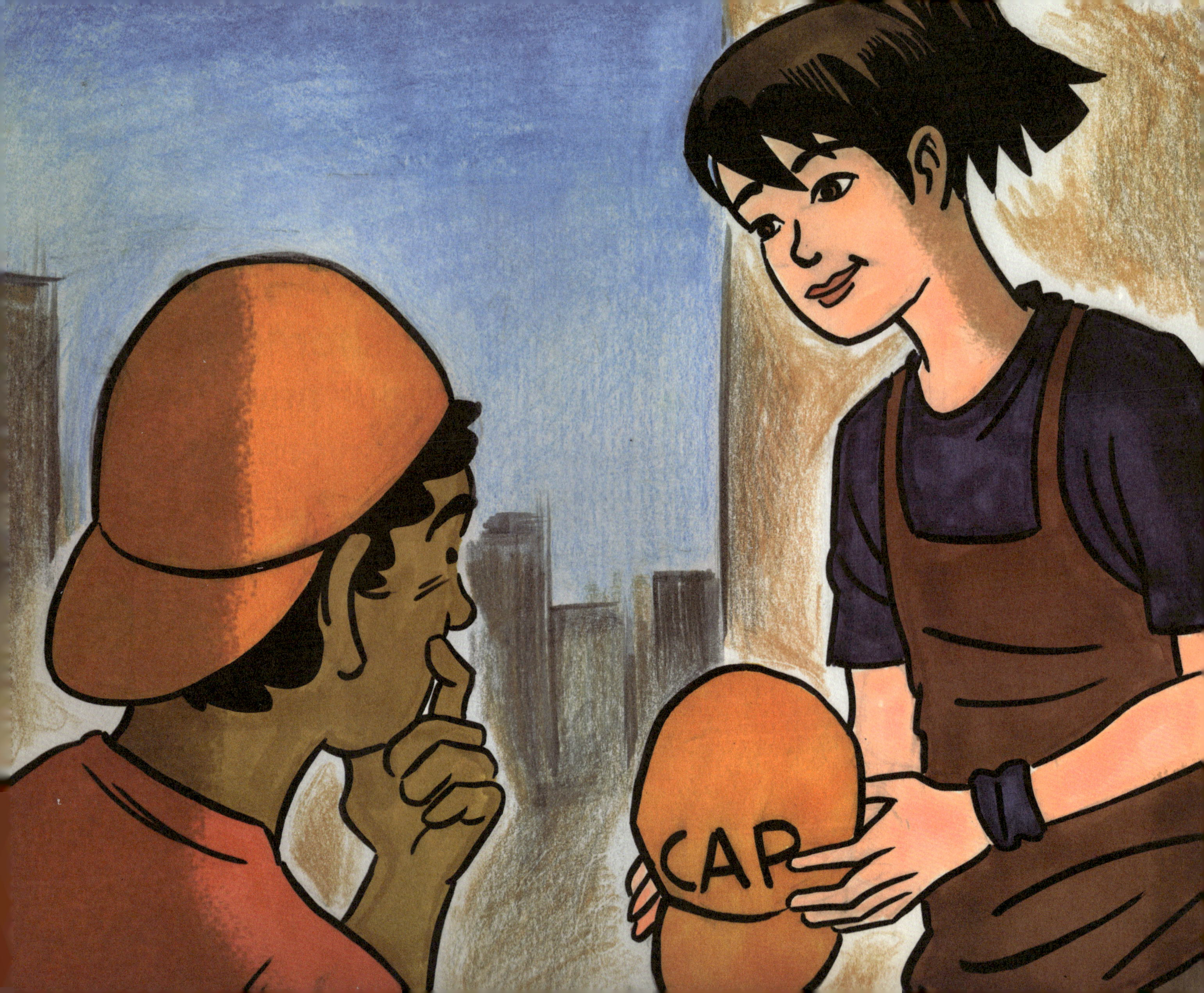
CAP

"The first letter on my CAP stands for 'cool,'" said Crystal. "When you threw your new glove you were NOT being cool. Cool players don't act crazy. Cool players take a deep breath, think about what they need to do to play better, and try hard the next time."

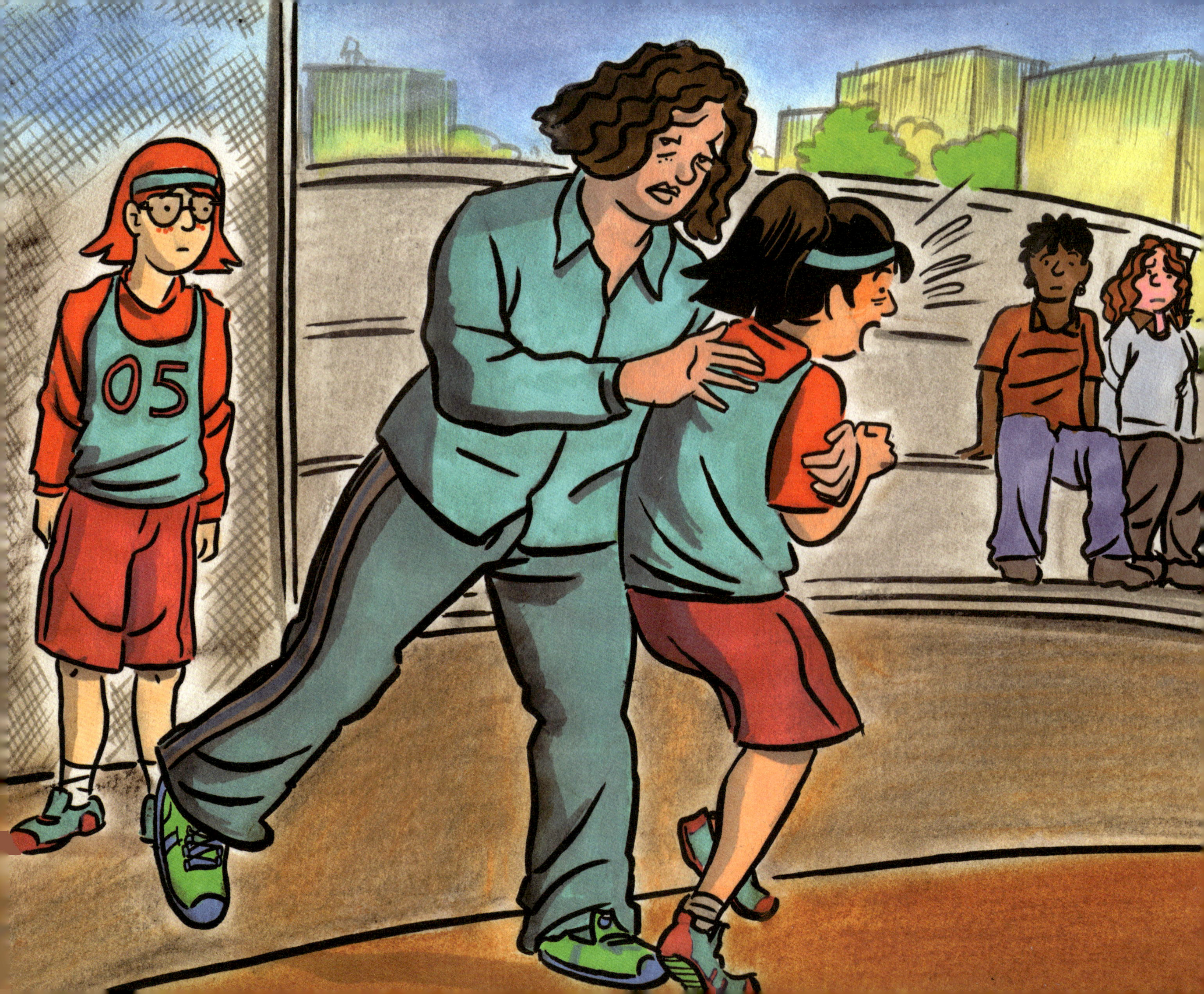
05

Crystal said, "I used to get so mad at basketball that Coach Chris would take me out of games. Coach Chris told me that if I learned how to use CAP, I would never have to miss a practice or a game because I was too angry."

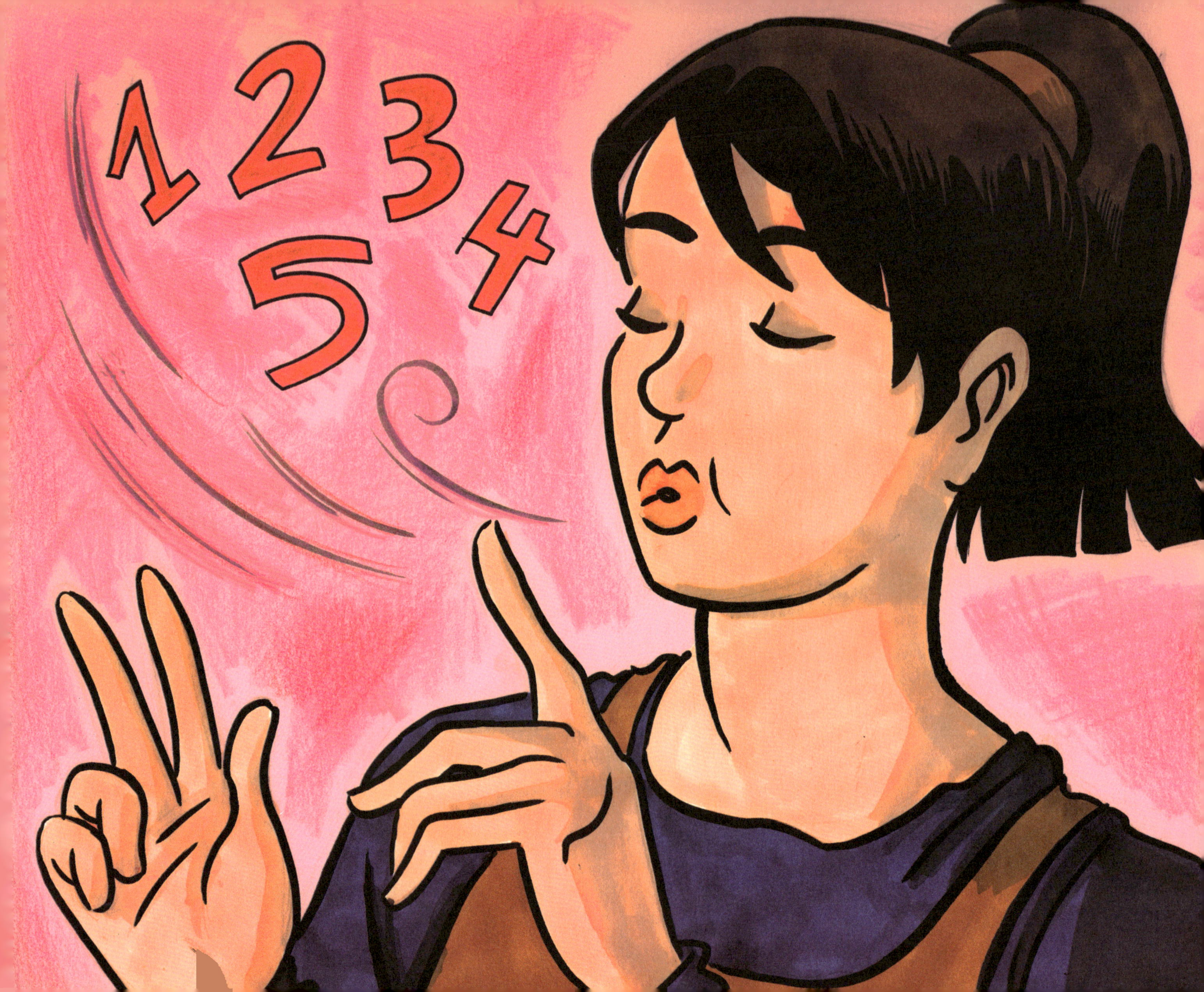
1 2 3 4 5

"To stay cool I breathe by the numbers. Let's practice. Take a deep breath through your nose and count slowly to four. Let the air fill up your stomach. Then, slowly let all the air come out from your mouth while you count to five. I breathe by the numbers at basketball and also if I get mad at school."

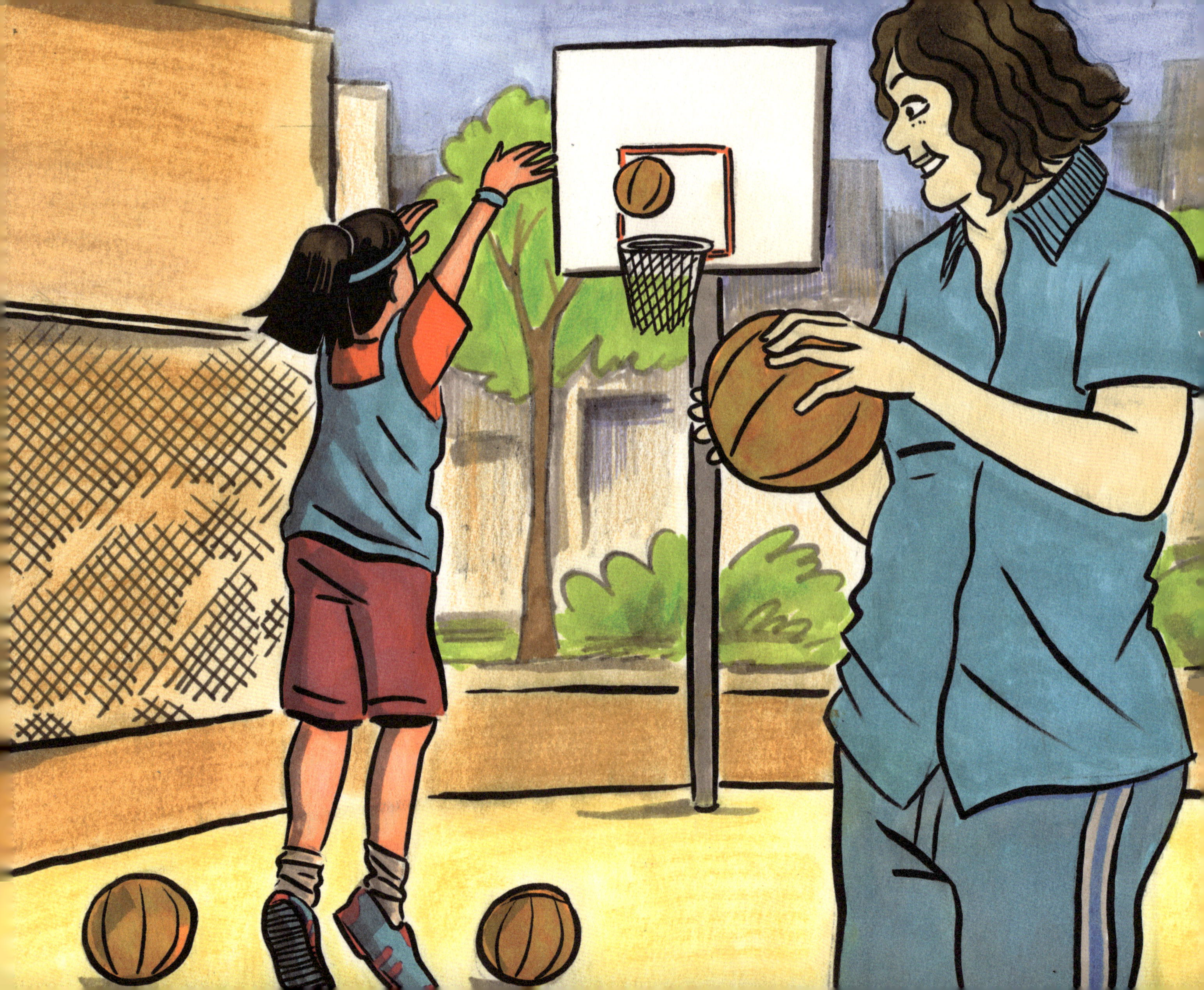

"The second letter in CAP, 'A,' stands for 'ask for help.' I asked my cousin, Rhonda to cheer for me and remind me when I need to stay cool. I asked Coach Chris to teach me some new dribbling and shooting drills."

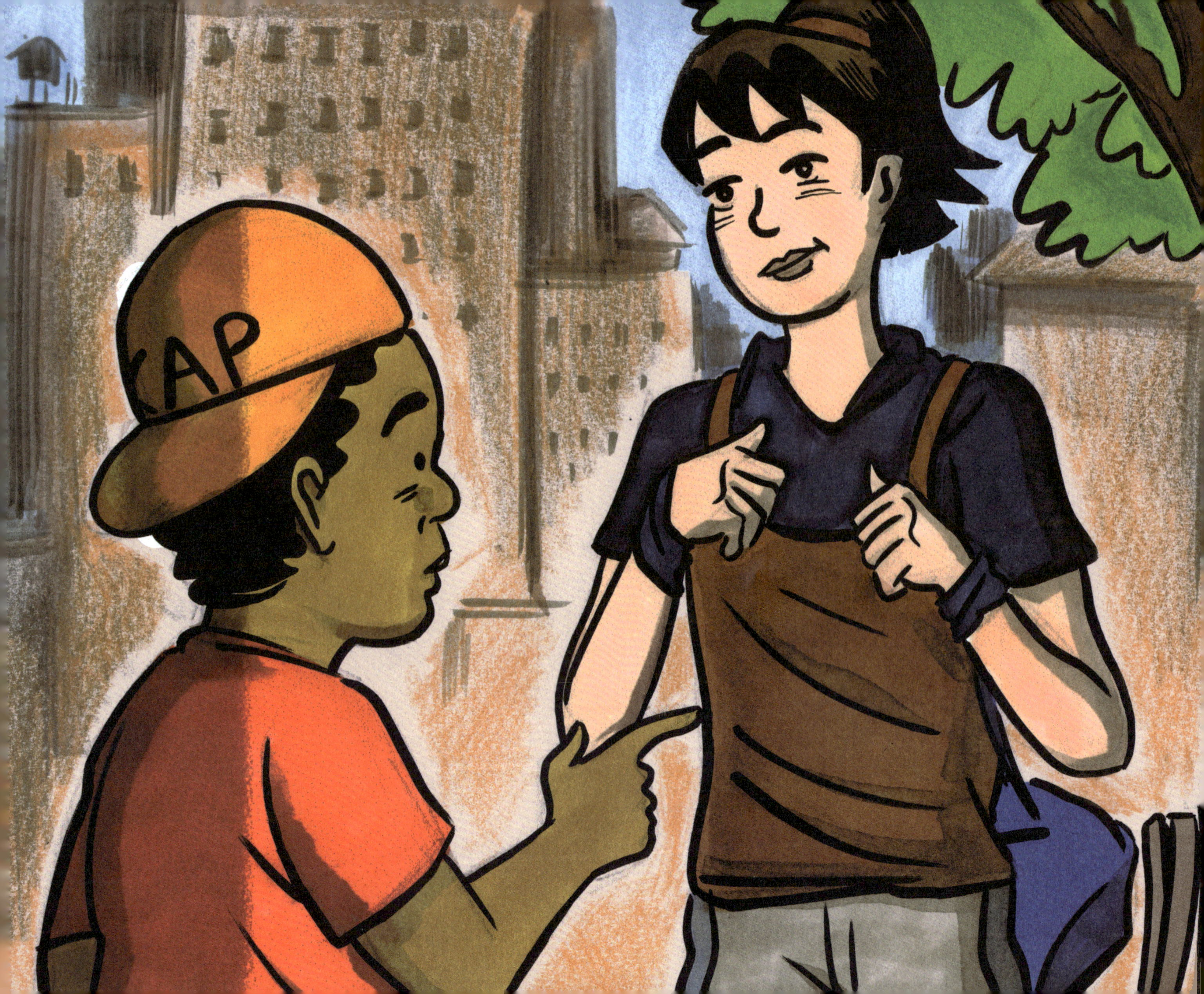
KAP

"Thanks, Crystal," I said. "I'm going to the tennis courts hitting wall to practice my game." "Wait!!" said Crystal. "Before you go, remember you need to find your own people to cheer you on and teach you new skills when you need help."

Guess who was the first person I asked to be on my support team. Yes, it was Crystal.

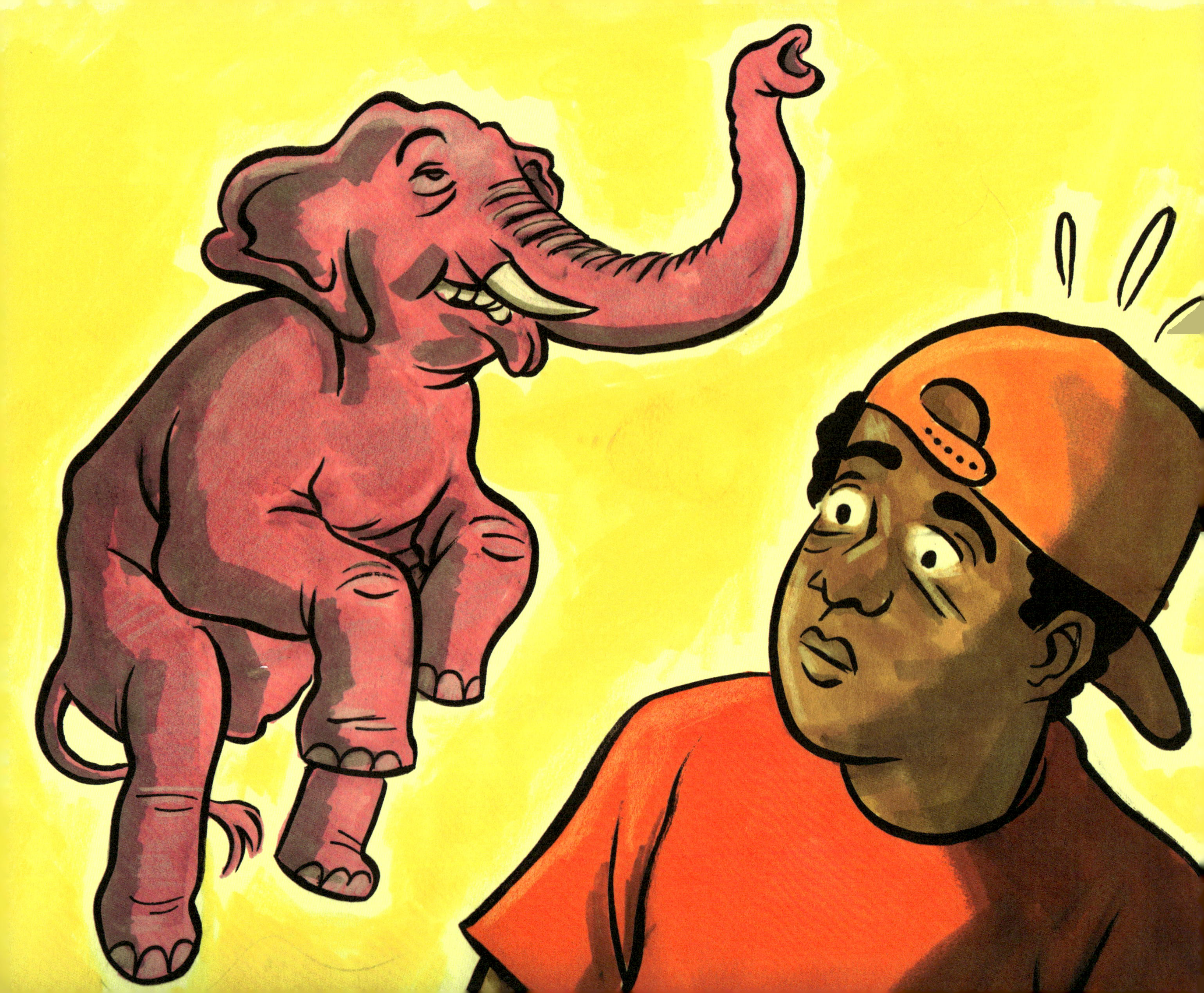

I started to run off. "Hey, Rudy," Crystal shouted, "Do **NOT** think about a pink elephant." Once she said **NOT** to think about it, a pink elephant popped into my mind.

It was like when I was playing baseball in the park. I was thinking, do **NOT** strike out and then I struck out. "Why did you say that, Crystal?" I asked. "Now I am all messed up!"

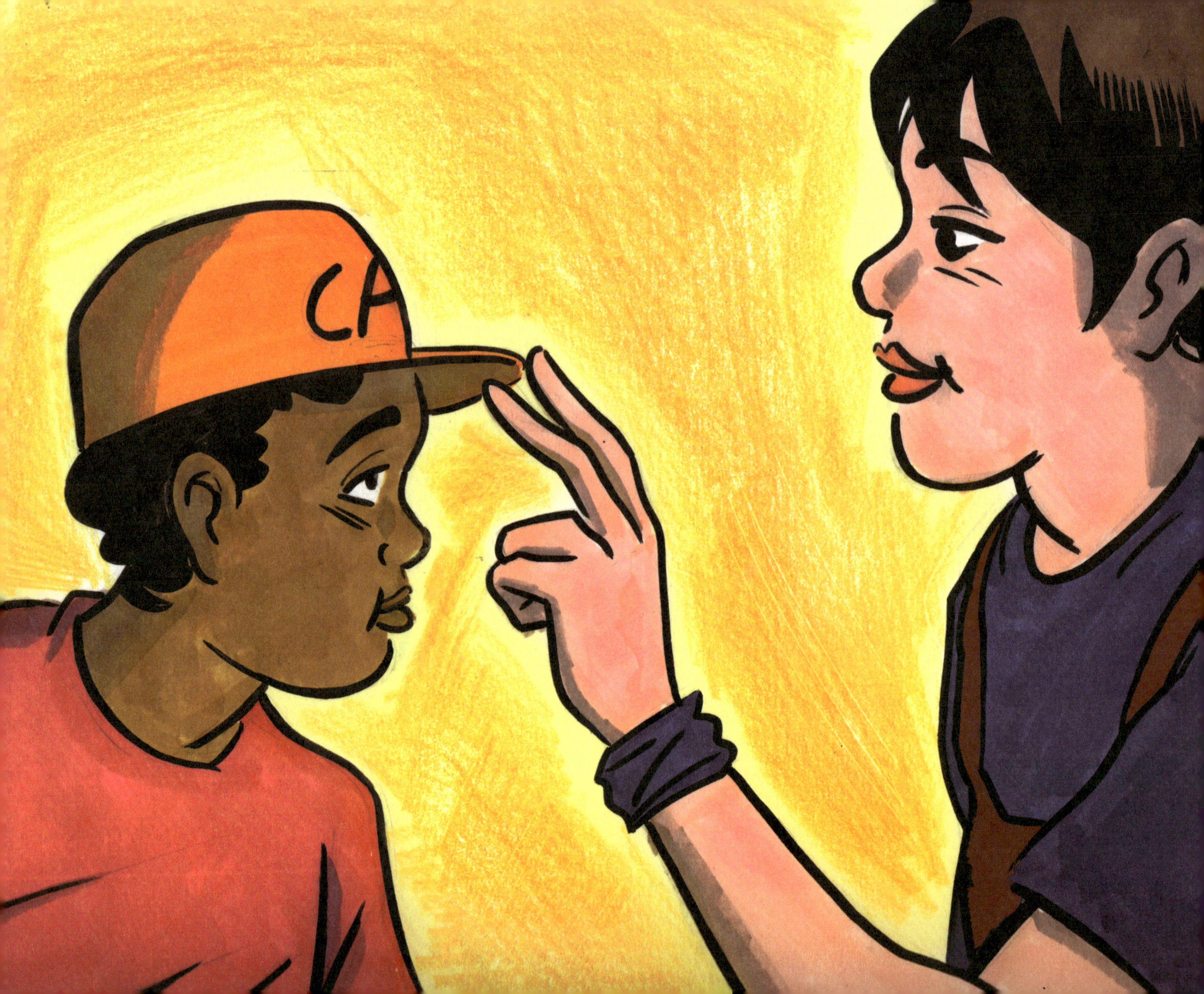
CA

"It's the last skill- the letter "P" in the secret CAP," she said. "It stands for think positive to play your best. Next time you are up at bat, focus on the ball and let your thoughts of pink elephants and striking out just fade away." Then Crystal gave me her CAP!

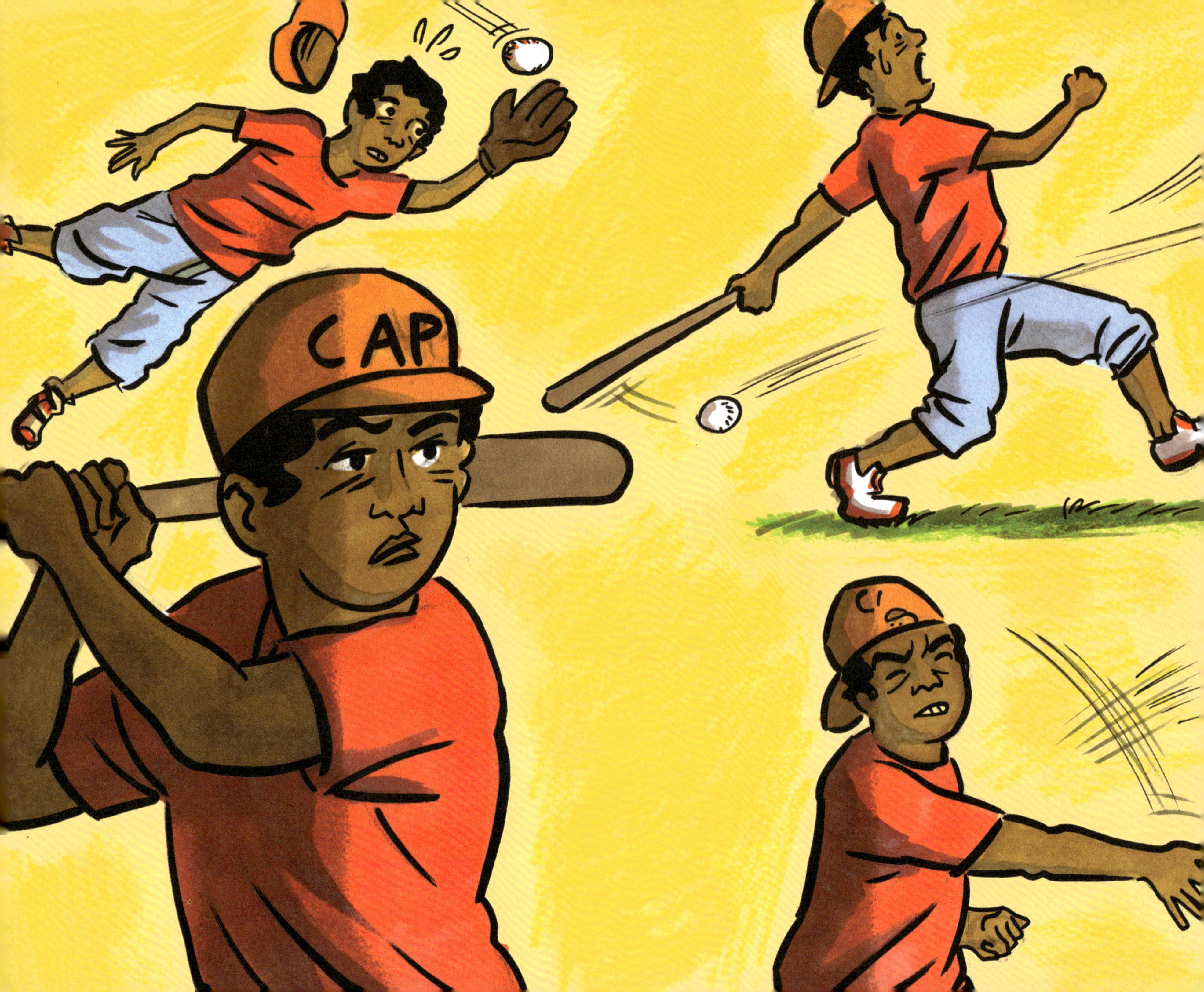
CAP

That summer I asked my friends and support team for help when I needed it. I learned to exercise, drink plenty of water, eat healthy foods, and practiced catching, hitting, and throwing.

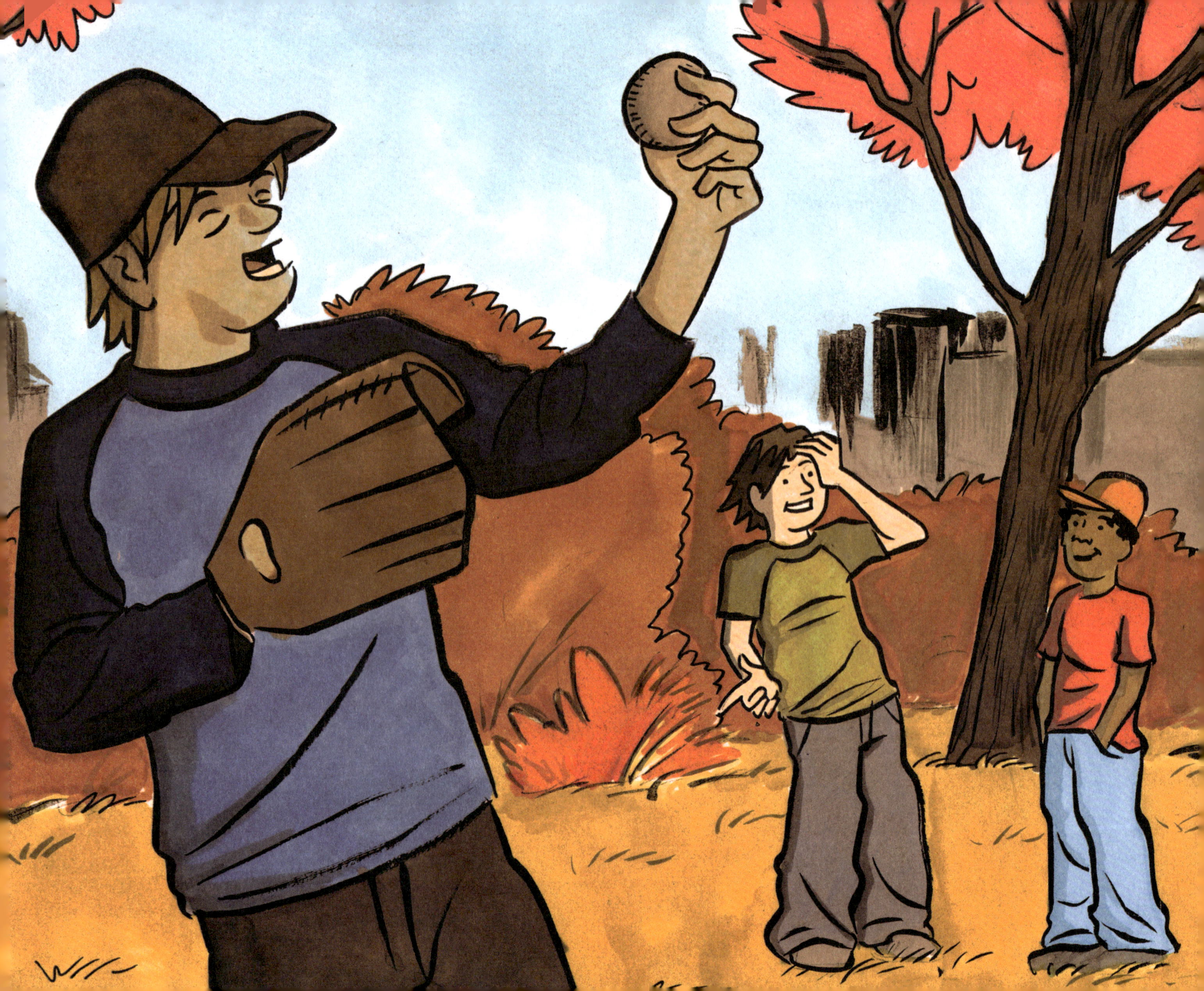

In the fall, I was back at the park. Carlos asked if I wanted to join the game. I grabbed my glove and my CAP and ran onto the field. My first time at bat, I made an out, but I used breathing by the numbers to stay cool.

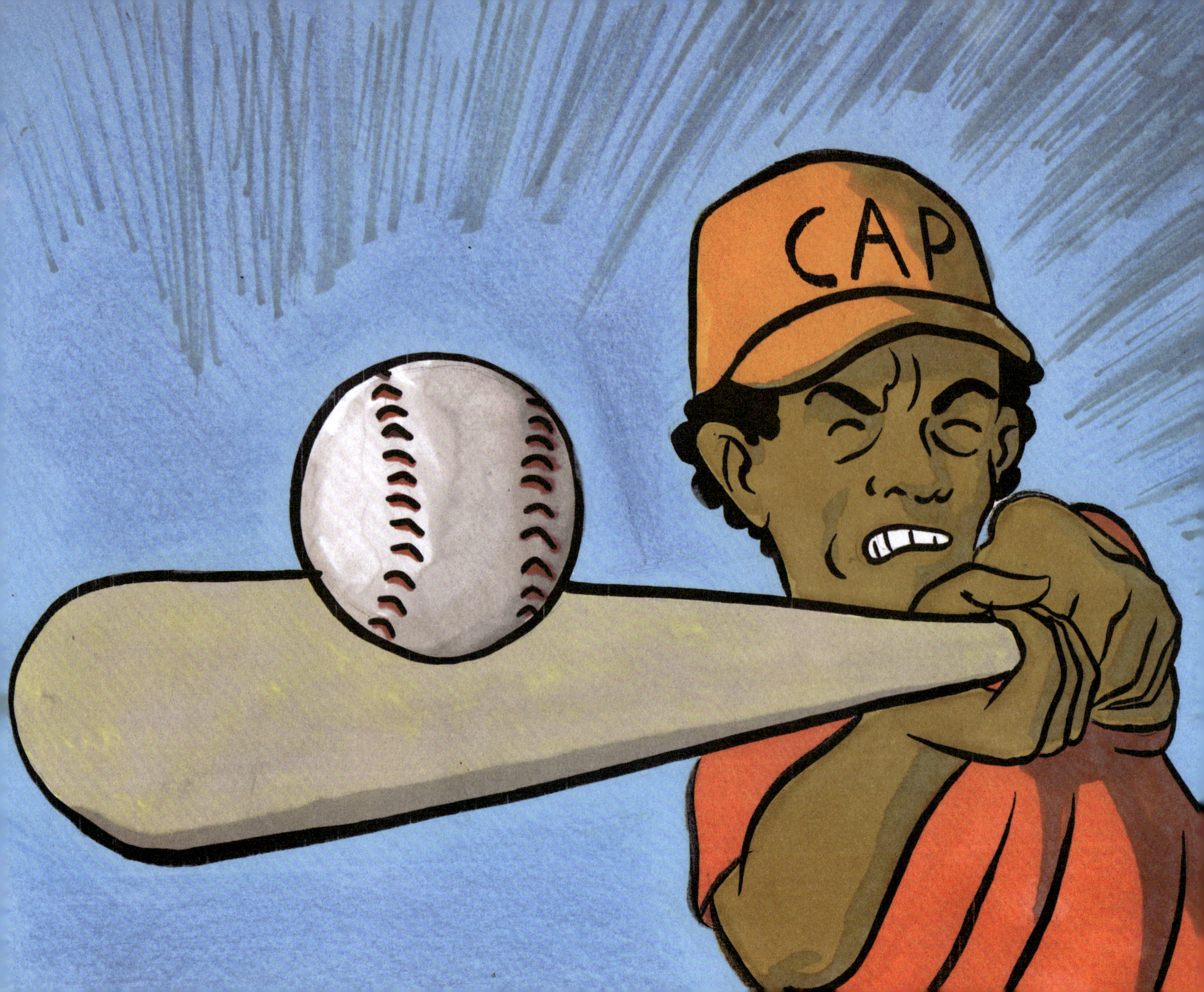
CAP

On my second at bat, I missed the first pitch, but stayed positive and focused on just hitting the ball. Then on the next pitch, I hit the ball over the third baseman's head and the ball rolled all the way to the fence. I kept running and rounded third base when I heard Carlos yell at me to run faster.

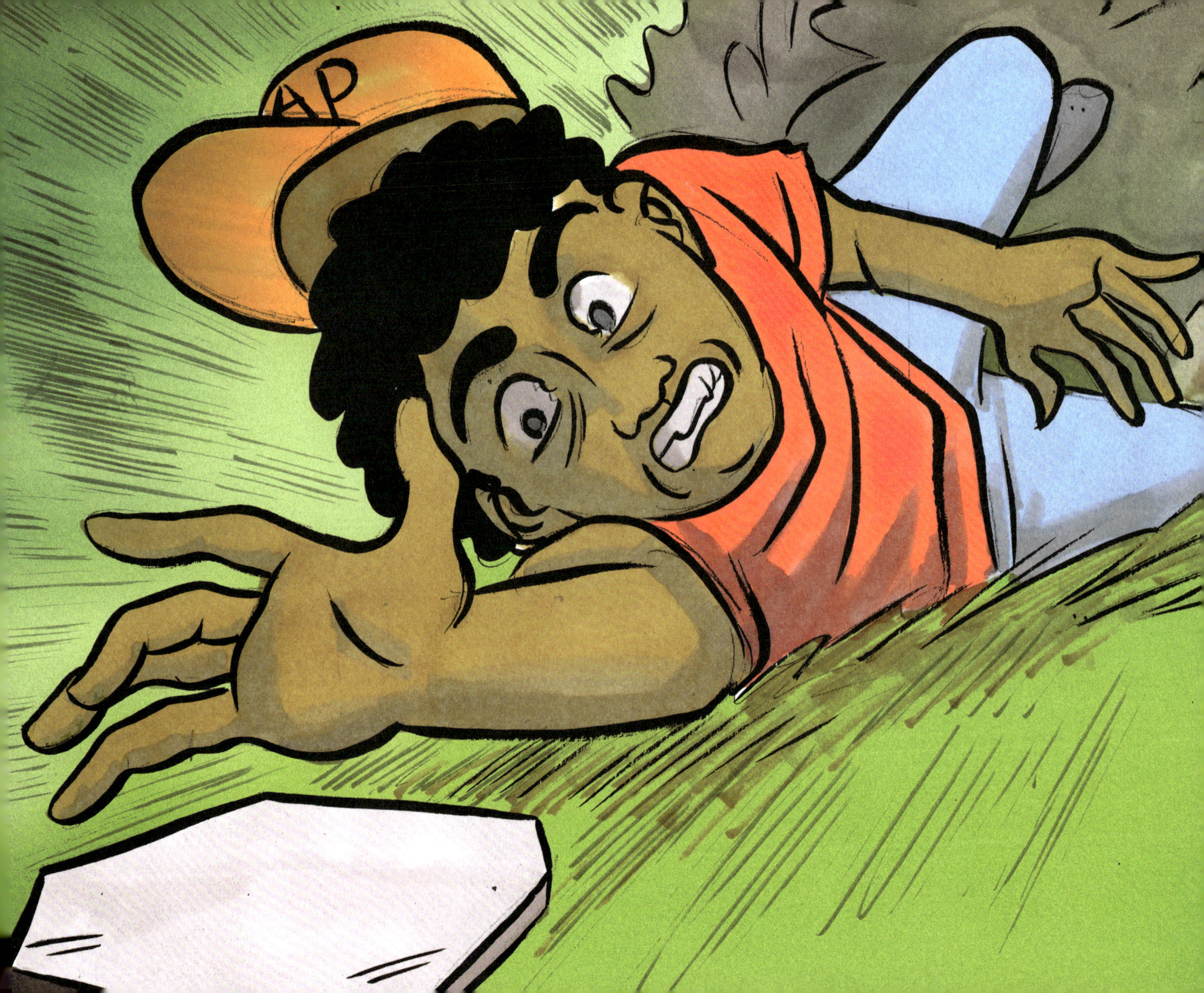
AP

As I got near home plate, Carlos yelled "slide!" With all my strength, I reached for home plate and slid home safe. I stood up and looked over at Carlos. He gave me a big smile. It was then that I realized how much I had improved.

In all the excitement, my CAP had fallen on the ground. I picked it up, shook off the dirt and put it back on my head. As I did, I thought about those three simple letters. Now, as I get ready to go to college, I know that if I remember to stay COOL, ASK for help, and focus on the POSITIVE, I will do my best in sports and in school.

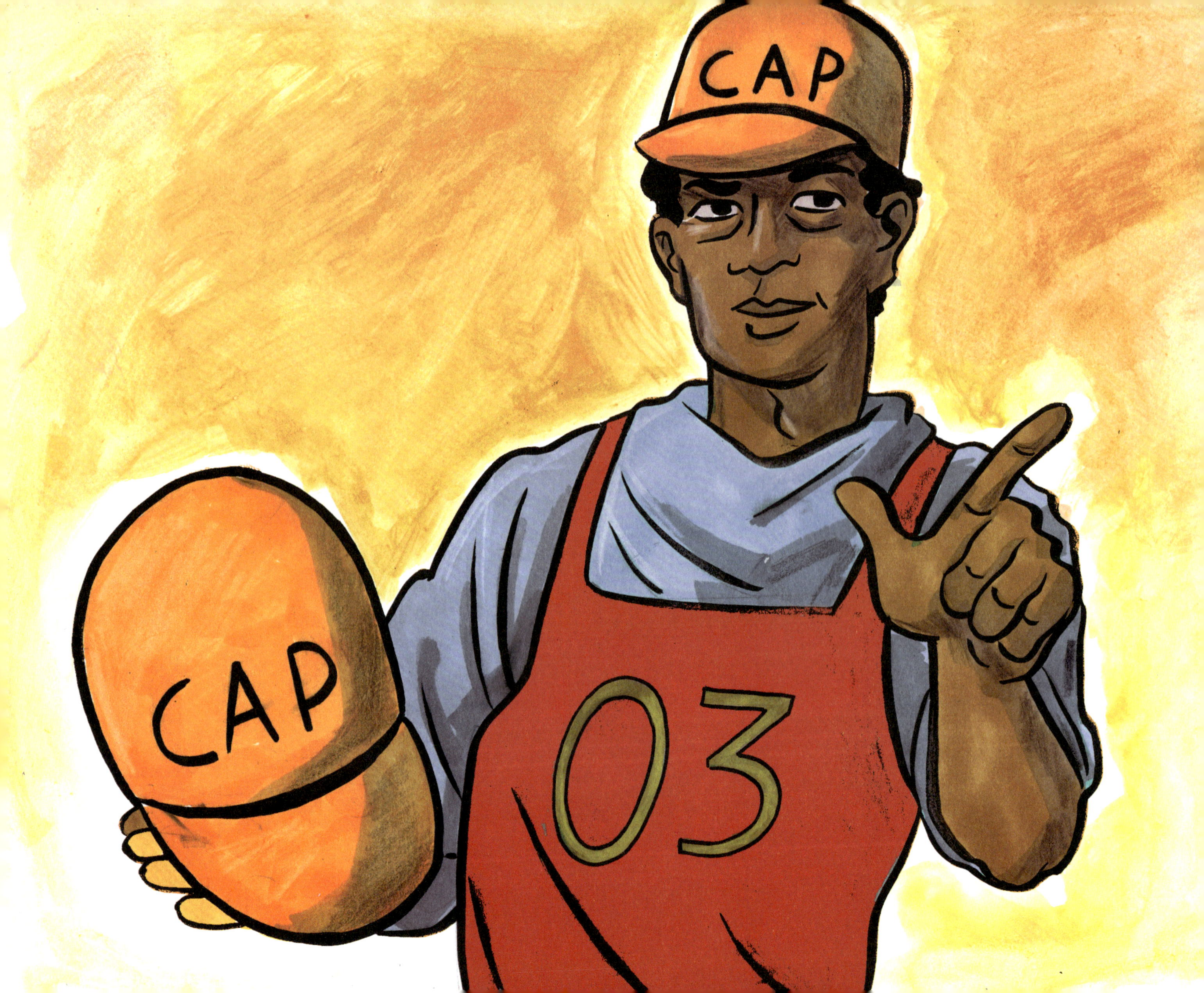
CAP
CAP
03